Finding Myself Postpartum

Brittney Bynum

BookLeaf Publishing

India | USA | UK

Presentation by *BookLeaf Publishing*

Web: www.bookleafpub.com

E-mail: info@bookleafpub.com

ISBN: 9789360940577

First edition 2024

To the person I am becoming. I am so proud of you.

ACKNOWLEDGEMENT

Thank you BookLeaf Publishing for this opportunity to process life through poetry. It's been an amazing adventure.

Something Bigger

There has to be something bigger than this,
A reason for it all,
God are you out there?
Please tell me these problems are small,

I need to hear your voice,
Tell me it's going to be okay,
Or take me home,
I don't mind either way,

If everything is for good,
Then you must have a plan from here,
Will you bring me joy on the other side?
O' Lord tell me if that time is near,

I am holding on to hope,
God, this is bigger than me,
I can do all things through you,
I just need fresh eyes to see,

I pray your kingdom is growing,
Make this pain have a purpose,
Show me what I need to do,
To carry this beating heart through,

God I need you now,
I will give you everything,
Just please promise you won't leave me,
Here fighting is so lonely.

"God Has Spoken"

Completely in shock,
Oh how long it lasted,
The pain was scary,
My soul tested,

You came as a surprise,
A girl your dad shouted,
Mommy motionless on the floor,
Thirty hours exhausted,

"Take your shirt off,"
Give her tummy time,
I need a minute,
To get out of this grime,

I stand weak as a tree branch in a storm,
Asking myself why I wasn't excited,
Your special day has arrived,
In shock –I am far from delighted,

Until we crawl into bed and
You lay on my chest,
My world stops again,
This time with you I feel completely blessed,

First time parents up all night,
Watching your chest with each breath,
We have so much to learn,
I promise baby girl, your love and trust we will
earn,

How did God create you so perfect and sweet,
Colic, binkies, bouncing and cutting teeth,
Every stage has been a miracle because of you,
The grace you have,
And the joy you bring is something entirely new,

I hope you grow to know,
You are so smart, strong-willed and beautiful,
There is so much about you to envy,
You will be a blessing to so many.

A Gift From God's Garden

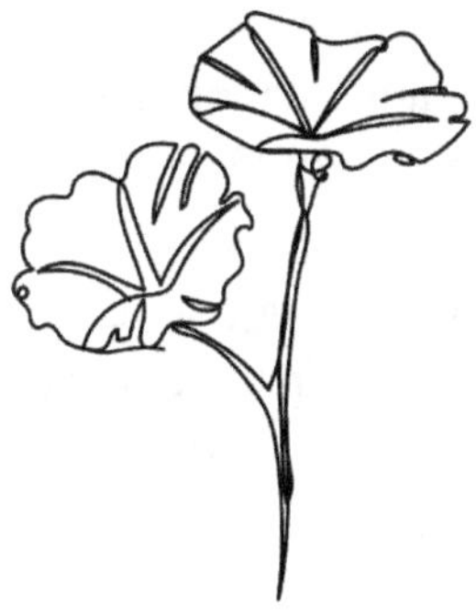

You were the gift I didn't know I needed,
The timing did not match my story,
God put you on my heart one day,
New Year's Eve we hugged warmly,

I wasn't ready to bring you into the world,
I don't know why God trusted me,
I was falling apart in every way,
God this cannot be correct I plea,

Carrying you was hard,
One of the hardest I have ever done,
No energy, growing pains, and fighting,
Nothing about this journey was fun,

Quit my job and moved away,
Trying to pave a path for you,
Are you sure I am the mom he needs,
How in the Hell will I handle TWO,

Ten at night contractions start,
It is you and me against the world,
Not a single bag is packed,
Baby you are coming in twelve hours to be
exact,

The pushing didn't stop,
Something about your shoulders,
I lost all my strength in your dad's arms I fall,
He cheers like it's a football game to give it my
all,

You made it to us two weeks early,
Dad nervous to hear your breath,
Mom hears them call out 30 seconds,
But mostly I'm just dizzy in the suspense,

You brought life back to me,
The son I wasn't sure I'd ever have,

God laughed at my plans,
And gave me the best child he had,

Your love is mighty though you may be small,
There is something so very special about it all,
I have God to thank every time I see your smile,
Someday I hope you understand,
You make my world worthwhile.

Grandma Someday

One day I will be a grandma,
One you can count on,
I will make a promise today,
I will never leave you astray,

I will be there when you need a nap,
Cook your favorite food,
I will hold your baby when you need a break,
As many as you need to take,

Hands-on with your kids,
They are safe with me,
Don't lose who you are,
Keep your God given beauty,

I want you to be the best version of yourself,
Don't ever hesitate to ask,
Do you need money or a place to sleep?
Or just my arms for a short weep?

If distance ever separates us,
You will never wait for my call,
You will always be on my mind,
I would do anything for you big or small,

I hope when I become a grandma,
I can give you all the love and support you need,
I want your kids to know me well,
And have stories they can forever tell,

It is my promise to you,
Your kids will feel my love,
Everyday I have the chance,
Until the day I am called above.

The Day God Made

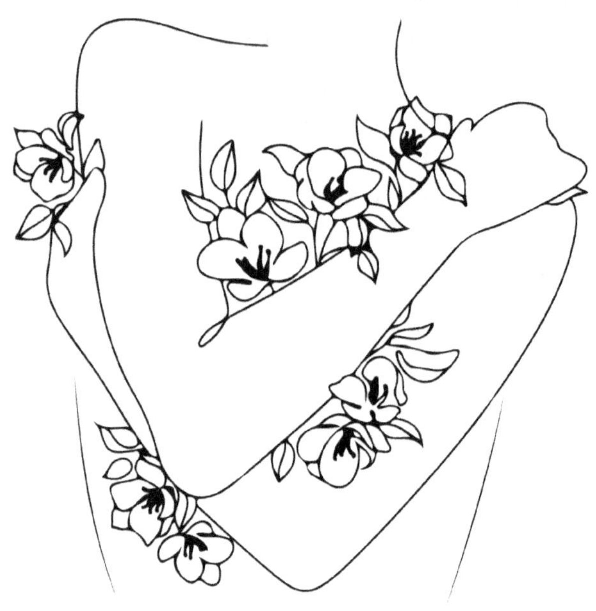

Sing to your coffee,
Seize the day,
Dance with your spatula,
It doesn't matter what anyone else has to say,
This day only comes once,
Make every moment beautiful,
Kids grow fast,
Keep being the music in their soul,
Make pancakes that smile back at you,

Sing songs that makes you groove,
Let hugs last forever,
This is a moment you do not want to lose,
Go outside for fresh air,
Give your kids a reason to smile,
Count your blessings big and small,
Pick flowers once in a while,
Speak beautiful things about others,
Love them near and far,
Sends gifts with lots of meaning,
And remember you already have it all.

Facing the Storm

If someone told you quitting was easy,
Have you ever tried to walk away?
Do you know how many pieces are in your
puzzle,
If you threw it all away?

The lives that are impacted,
Far exceed your own,
You think hard about your actions,
Before you step down from your throne,

It is easier to place blame on others,
Than to look at ourselves objectively,
Who is really the problem,
It takes more than one person ultimately,

Growing is always the answer,
Show the next generation how,
Healing is the right thing to do,
You will not always feel the way you do now,

Let your negative emotions out,
Stop giving them power,
Change your perspective,
Take it hour by hour,

You have to forgive and find a way to move on,
Don't hold on to animosity for long,
Set your mind free of hate and keeping score,
Drop people in your life who don't make you
strong,

Before you throw it all away,
Remember this,
Life is a precious gift,
And you will need love to get through it.

Just as a Snake Sheds Its Skin

The person I used to be,
Trying to fight hard for what she believed,
Always second guessing,
But the world is ready for a new me,

I used to fear if I was a good mom,
I took to heart everyone's advice,
Hearing "You hold her too much" was the norm,
I know they thought they were just being nice,

I've since learned I am the best at loving my
own babies,
Your comments I no longer live by,
We do not swaddle, use gripe water, and cosleep,
I do not feel I need to explain why,

I want my life to be about supporting other
moms,
Believe you are the best of your kind,
Screen time is not going to define their life,
Hold on to your piece of mind,

I used to think every day needed to be perfect,
On my A game,

Then I realized my kids are watching how we
love one another,
And clean dishes or quality time are certainly
not the same,

Slow down and watch how they get stronger
each day,
Keep your expectations in line,
Soon they will be walking,
Even behind Google's schedule it is the perfect
time,

Your baby will survive a small bonk,
You were not irresponsible,
You will get frustrated and yell once or twice,
Mama your growth is remarkable,

Listen to others' opinions but don't let it define
you,
You don't need to worry about, I told you so,
Critics will see them thrive and already know,
Your loyalty to your kids is all that you owe.

Forever Together

There will be a day you only have each other,
Mom and dad not around any longer,
My heart desires that you stay close,
And every moment together you grow stronger,

Spend the holidays together,
Cherish each others kids,
Carry on traditions,
So they can last forever,

Never pass up the opportunity to call,
Never let a week go by,
Without sending the other a smile,
You are both worth the extra mile,

Never lose your urge to dance,
Pray over one another,
Mama will always follow in spirit,
Seize every opportunity given the chance,

I want you both to have the help that you need,
Childcare, money, food, or space to breath,
I am counting on you to show up unannounced,
And be the blessing the other needs,

When you feel you have nothing left,
And you can't hear it from me,
Remind one another,
You only need the faith of a mustard seed—it
will set you free.

Who am I Without You

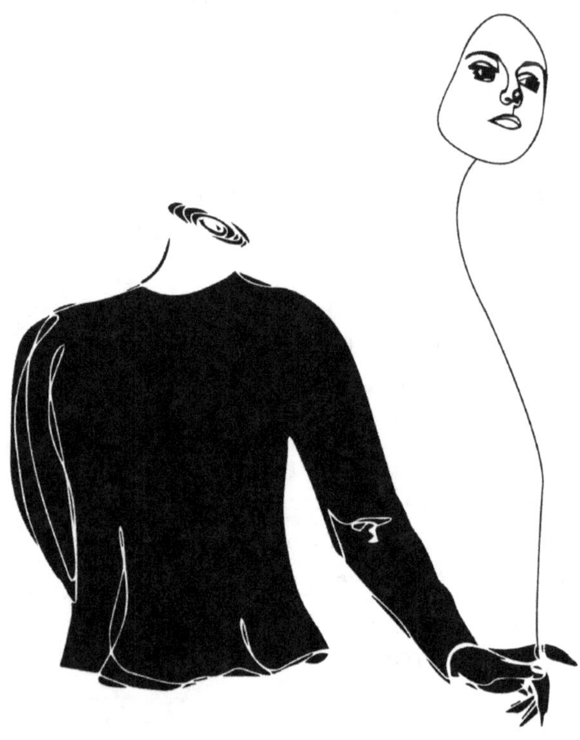

When I was born my life was about being a little
sister,
Loved and cherished by many,
My sister's dream come true,
Enjoying her different forms of entertainment
were plenty,

When I turned six my life was about me,
Learning to read, cherish friends, and Barbies,
I was intelligent above many,
Never skipping a chance to play across the
street,

In high school life was about learning to love,
Losing friends over drama to regain them
stronger in the end,
First relationships that gave you butterflies,
Only to leave you cheated and on a path to
mend,

When I hit college life was about adventure,
Camping, road trips, and all around fun,
Pizza breaks with friends by day—swimming
and drinks by night,
You could find us trying new things everyday
around the sun,

Single life I was number one,
I read books, slept in and had quiet peaceful
meals,
Hair always made, tight fitting clothes, and
prioritizing nails being done,

Married life was about learning someone else's
way,
How we brush our teeth was different,

Sleeping habits, cleaning, and how we structured
the day,
Down to even the things we would say,

Having a baby is when it all was lost,
Who am I today?
My phone doesn't ring,
I do not go out,
I'm covered in barf,
And my hair is falling out,

To say that things changed would be an
understatement,
When I look in the mirror,
I do not know the person looking back,
And it's starting to become clear,
The person I used to be is no longer here,

Will she ever play darts like before?
Will she still garden, lift weights, and travel
galore?
Please bring her back she was so fun,
She knew what she stood for and didn't settle for
anyone,
She was hard headed and knew how to be happy,
Who am I now, why does it feel so different to
be me?

The Lies We Believe

He will hold the door,
Hug you from behind,
He will bring you fresh roses,
Love is always kind,

He will text you sweet messages,
Throughout his busy day,
And will be over the moon to see you,
When he takes off his shoes in the doorway,

Love is not easily angered,
And it definitely is not rude,
You will feel seen for everything you do,
He will show mercy on the hard days you barely
make it through,

Or maybe just maybe,
That is what they led us to believe,
But your reality is different,
In the love that you receive,

You cry yourself to sleep,
When it matters the most,
He doesn't have time,
To hear what you have to boast,

Your anxiety is high,
Is he really telling the truth,
Time will tell,
Or is this just another lie,

Will you be met with anger today,
Should you lock yourself away,
Remember to go easy,
He had a long day,

Don't mind your own feelings,
They are never okay,
Navigate the discouragement and insults,

But keep your own comments at bay,

Pick your head up,
Seething or sad,
Nobody is there to see the day you had,

If you think you'll get help,
Darling you are wrong,
Because no one is allowed to know,
Not family, not friends, it's not the business of
anyone.

Touched Out

Please don't touch me ever so slightly,
It's been a long day with you in my arms,
I know it is confusing the way that I am,
I hug you, squeeze you and hold you all day,
Then at night "leave me alone" is all you hear
me say,

I love you so very much,
It's nothing that you did,
But the feeling of being touched out is so vivid,

I love your snuggles and kisses too,
But right now it feels like such a big ask,
Being alone is all I crave to do,

The guilt is overwhelming,
I know this phase goes fast,
I want to soak up every minute with you,
Oh please do not let this feeling last,

I take a break in the tub,
Wanting to crave you again,
All I see are your hands under the door,
You do not understand why you cannot have me anymore,

My body is no longer mine,
It serves you all hours of daylight,
I just need a minute to be me,
Then I can come back and make everything alright.

♡♡♡

Lonely Doesn't Mean Alone

I am lonely but not alone,
I wake up with ambition,
Then get intimidated,
When I realize it's just me on this mission,

You can write in your journal,
It's a substitute for crying on a shoulder,
When you talk out loud,
And the people in the room are not in your
corner,

The conversations are shallow,
My personality is deeper than that,
But only if you have the right company,
Or learn to bear the silence with a laugh,

There is a room full now,
Hoping someone will appreciate you,
The amazing spirit you have,
Coming out of your shell is hard to do,

Lonely doesn't mean you are the only one there,
It's a feeling that no one cares,
So you learn to keep to yourself,
It's not worth the energy it takes to share,

You keep going and pretend your needs are
getting met,
Praying for an angel,
God is listening don't you fret,
But deep down you are lonely.

Dirty Thirty

I want to meet someone new,
I want our kids to play,
I make an effort to reach out,
Let's be friends, what do you say?

Library dates to read out loud,
Coffee to laugh and bond,
Playgrounds galore,
If I could just wish and wave a wand,

I want to do these things with you,
I was always so outgoing,
And I crave connection,
A friend who laughs in photos of us glowing,

I wake up with less energy than the wind,
I don't check my phone often,
How would I ever hold a friendship,
If hearing from me becomes foreign,

Kids always come first,
I want to show them how fun it can be,
I just don't know how to push through the chaos,
To spend a day that's not just you and me,

Mommy is trying to overcome the fatigue,
We have people to see,
Each day I have hope it doesn't show its face,
And there are a million better things to do than
sit at our place,

Zipfizz, sleep, encouraging words and coffee,
I cannot seem to get a grip—it is harder than it
looks,
Making friends at this age,
Doesn't happen like you read in the books.

New Ambition

It is the new year,
Thirteen wishes on my radar,
It is time to reflect,
And wish upon a star,

Twelve out of my control,
One for me to indulge,
Without God I am powerless,
Praying big this year he is generous,

I wished for a business,
A career change is not far,
I wished for a hobby,
Maybe yoga, dancing, or Barre,

I wished for more connection,
Deeper love like Jesus our king,
I wished for some self-help,
Maybe some direction God will bring,

Not sure what I am destined to do,
But there is a Father with a plan,
Walking, waiting, wishing to see,
What he finds worthy of thee,

I wished to learn something new,
Bake sourdough,
Learn a craft,
Maybe monetize on Youtube,

Being a better person for my family—
Would be a dream come true,
You know what they say if you shoot for the
moon,
I pray to find fruit from these goals someday
soon.

Thessalonians–Walking Idle

The open arms you never gave,
The tune of my drum,
You set out to drain,
The drugs you took to hide the pain,

You truly hurt people,
Accountability will never be had,
You hide behind the idea of faith,
Not the drugs that you had,

You want to be relevant,
But you just don't know how,
The corner you occupy,
Never present in the here and now,

The guilt you place on others,
How awful can you be,
The entitlement you have,
I hope someday the devil will set you free,
Ultimately the family that will never be,
Because you just can't accept me.

Distracted

Is it more important than me,
Whatever you can see through that screen,
The trick I just did jumping off the couch,
Did you even see?

My childhood in the making,
Idle,
Out of touch with reality,

The little attention I receive,
Lacking its genuinity,
What is so important behind that screen?

I have a lot of energy,
I just want to share these memories with you,
It seems to me football is not going to be the one
to wait,
Can I sit and watch whatever you do?

I like to draw pictures,
To bring a smile to your face,
Though they look better on the wall,
With your nose behind that electronic device,

I would love if you taught me to kick the soccer
ball,
Or even if I could show you my gymnastics
backbend,
I know you do not mean to be absent,
But I am little and don't understand why I take
second,

Why don't you put your phone away,
Today can be our special day,
We can get to know each other better,
And it will show me that I truly matter,

Unless you don't have time,
I will play independently,
And grow to learn,
The screens come first inevitably.

My Little Shadow

You make me proud,
With so much love for life,
The way you try new things,
The personality you share so loud,

The way you encourage your friends,
Your hugs that can stop time,
The way you take charge,
How brave you are is almost a crime,

You are such an amazing athlete,
Always ready to pave the way,
Every summersault, jump and kick make me
smile,
The mismatched socks you proudly wear in
style,

The way you never fear to swim,
The slides, the lazy rivers and vacations,
You seize every opportunity you get,
Eager to take life by the horns on a whim,

I pray you never slow down,
I cannot express how much potential you
exhibit,
Fiercely chase what brings you joy,
The spirit God gave you is exquisite!

The Gift That Keeps on Giving

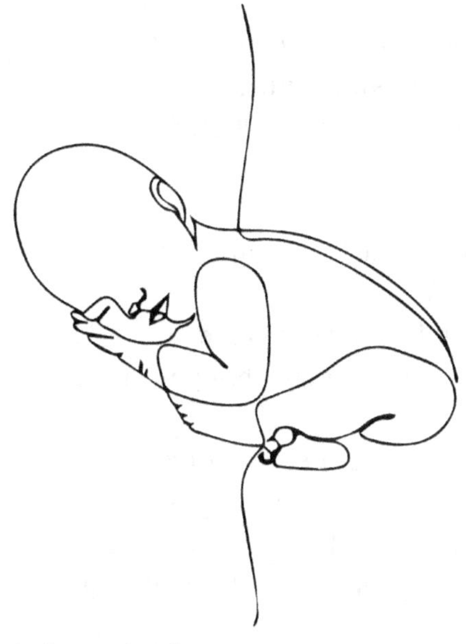

The pain in my boobs,
God gave me to sustain life,
Cluster feeding through the night,
Your future is so bright,

Stop what I am doing,
I am a slave to your cry,
Home twenty-four seven,
In 9 months we will kiss it goodbye,

We should use this time to bond,
Cuddle and sing songs,
Your farm noises are sweet,
But the deed I'm not fond,

I love you to the moon,
I know it is worthwhile,
The spit up stains you share,
I wear in classic mom style,

Leaking through my shirt,
Where did my baby go,
When did these teeth come in,
It is amazing just how fast you grow,

It's time you start eating solids,
Mommy is going to wean you slow,
I look at you so healthy and strong,
Wondering why it feels terribly wrong,

These days I reminisce,
As weak and weary as they made me,
As a distant memory they make me teary.

Leaving Feels Impossible

How do I turn around and walk away,
Knowing the only person you want is me,
I'm growing more overwhelmed by the day,
I need some time with my hands free,

Mentally it's the right thing to do,
Setting self-care as a priority,
Physically I'm ill passing you into another set of
arms,
I truly cannot be without you,

I try to get some exercise,
My mind is racing like a horse track,
Should I just go peek in the window?
Severely fighting the urge to go back,

Do you laugh and play while I'm gone?
I wonder what crosses your mind,
Mama's anxiety is above and beyond,
Are your teachers one of a kind?

I'm coming back to get you,
I can't take this anymore,
Your resilience is admirable,
But mommy is going to keep you close
forevermore.

Ayurvedic Acrostic

Power in the words that we say,
Once they come out their legacy stays,
We choose wisely to use them for good or
bad—build your kids up,
Every chance that you have,
Remember when you were being raised,
Once upon a time,
Foul language and ridicule truly broke you
down,
Words can surely hurt long after their sound,
Of course things can be different now,
Realize the power is within you,
Don't let your anger win the race,
Say sorry and communicate with dignity and
grace.

Uniquely You

I don't know how to make it through,
Knowing the only person that can feed the baby
is you,
Tired, hurting and you've had enough,
Pulling through these times are tough,

Why do I feel like it's my fault,
Your tongue ties creating challenges from the
start,
How can I be the one letting you down,
I cannot handle the guilt of your frown,

God, am I broken?
Will his speech be altered when spoken?
Will he get teased by peers?
Will this be a lifetime of tears?

Moms have an innate yearning to protect,
Bring comfort and joy to their kin,
Not feeling adequate to feed feels in our soul
like neglect,
Believing these lies of the devil is the ultimate
sin.

You made me believe the procedure was simple,
It will take less than five minutes,
I give my consent,
But you advise me I cannot be present,

You close four doors between my baby and I,
I gaze through the tiny window holding back a
giant sigh,

My baby is swaddled tight,
Not able to put up a fight,

He doesn't know where mom is,
Is she praying that I am alright?

You are bleeding when I see you,
You don't want to eat,
For the first time I do not know what to do,
So we cuddle in the front seat,

It takes weeks of me pushing on your wounds,
Your scream brings me to my knees,
Someone send me strength,
Through these tears I need it please,

This was the right thing to do,
I tell myself over and over,
If only my heart felt that too,
These are the only memories of you,
That I hope someday my mind can lose.

Overwhelmed and Undervalued

Sleep when the baby sleeps,

Was not the advice for moms with multiple kin,

How will I get everything clean,

I feel like I cannot win,

Two-and-a-half months since the bathroom has
seen a mop,

Things are turning into good and bad cop,

Trying to get through the day without keeping
score,

But you just slept in,

Enjoyed a hands-free meal,

And used the bathroom alone,

I have a baby chair by the toilet,
I've learned to hold one baby on each hip,
I am peeling eggs with one hand,
Losing hope in my one man band,

Choose between getting dishes done,
Or the kids having any fun,
When do I get some relief,
Or even twenty minutes of sleep,

Do you understand how it feels,
When mom is always the only option,
The baby is content without dad,
All I can think to myself,
He really isn't half that bad!

Three is Company

You might be my last baby,
It makes me sad to say,
My heart wants more,
But my head thinks it doesn't want to be poor,

We don't have a tribe to help us through the
fight,
Just mommy and daddy with no village in sight,
This might be the price we pay
To make sure your future is happy and healthy
some day,

I hold you extra close,
Knowing this might be my last,
The smell of you is intoxicating,
How will this all become the past,

I know I do not get any sleep,
And quite frankly I am cranky,
I want to fully cherish these days,
It is difficult knowing baby coos and laughs will
only be a video replay,

One baby was hard,
Two almost broke me,
I like to believe I can love another,
I see myself as a superhuman mother,

But reality is not lost on me,
I want you both to have the world,
If three were to jeopardize that dream,
A third baby we will never see.

Time Passes By

When looking back,
You'll hear time goes fast,
That is not the whole story though,
Because the days in between truly go slow,

Diapers, nap, bath, and food,
On repeat all day through,
It does not feel there is an end in sight,
Every single task a new battle to fight,

Your babies are only small for a short time,
These are the days they tell us to enjoy,
But do they forget how tiring they can be,
When all I have is you and all you have is me,

Is it Monday, Tuesday, or Thursday today?
They all feel more or less the same,
Is there a holiday or special event coming?
Even a phone call or play date would feel
fulfilling,

It's not that I don't love you with my whole soul,
Or savor the time as it goes,
But my energy stores are empty,
And the mental toll is hefty,

Every 24 hours has a story,
Some a struggle and some ideal,
If this isn't your best chapter don't worry,
Raising kids is an entire journey.